ELEVATOR SPEECHES
that get results

PRAISE FOR
ELEVATOR SPEECHES THAT GET RESULTS

"Written for people who see themselves as introverts or socially reluctant, this book makes an intelligent contribution to the discussion of networking, an activity of dramatically increasing importance for personal stability in an increasingly uncertain professional world."

Martin Yate, CPC
NEW YORK TIMES BEST-SELLING AUTHOR,
"KNOCK EM DEAD–
SECRETS & STRATEGIES FOR SUCCESS IN AN UNCERTAIN WORLD"

"Dorothy Tannahill Moran hits the nail on the head in her book, ELEVATOR SPEECHES THAT GET RESULTS. *In this quick, easy read, I gained a deeper appreciation for the Elevator Speech as a tool for managing my personal brand. This little gem not only offers suggestions for how to use a well-crafted Elevator Speech, but also provides helpful tips for creating one, if not several. I especially appreciated her insight into what works and doesn't work in creating and delivering an Elevator Speech and have been inspired to rewrite my own. Well done!"*

Kristen Clark
CONFIDENCE COACH, AWARD-WINNING AUTHOR, EDITOR, PUBLISHER

"Being an IT Administrator, great ideas to help improve that efficiency of our systems are always in need, but not always easy to get across. In Dorothy's book it covers all areas and aspects of a speech you may need to work on. It is to the point, easy to understand, but not too oversimplified. This book has really helped me further my ideas and I highly recommend it to anyone who has problems getting their ideas across."

Randy Kennedy
AMAZON REVIEWER

"Fantastic book by a fantastic author. Highly recommend, no matter what field you're in or what personality type you are."

Justin Grabouski
AMAZON REVIEWER

the publishing CIRCLE

admin@ThePublishingCircle.com
or
THE PUBLISHING CIRCLE
Regarding: Dorothy Tannahill-Moran
19215 SE 34th Street
Suite 106-347
Camas, Washington 98607

ELEVATOR SPEECHES THAT GET RESULTS: CREATE A 30-SECOND INTRODUCTION FOR GREATER SUCCESS / DOROTHY TANNAHILL-MORAN
ISBN-978-1-947398-99-3

Book design by Michele Uplinger
Illustrations ©The Noun Project

ELEVATOR SPEECHES
that get results

Create a
30-second introduction
for greater success

Get Free Instant Access to Video series

"The 5 Most Common Ways Introverts Commit Career Self-Sabotage and How to Avoid Them"

These videos are designed to accelerate your results with **ELEVATOR SPEECHES THAT GET RESULTS,** and are my way of saying "thank you" for purchasing this book.

www.introvertwhisperer.com/careergoals

Contents

Foreword

IS IT JUST ME OR have you ever noticed that there are some things that get talked about but never seriously defined or laid out so that you know EXACTLY what those things are or how to do them? That was the situation with the "Elevator speech". When I first started to seriously pay attention to it, I discovered that most people acted like they collectively knew what an Elevator Speech was, but no one wanted to admit that they had no clue what they were talking about. It reminded me of the story of the emperor who had no clothes. Everyone went along with the scam until finally a person blew the whistle and asked where the emperor's clothes were.

That was myself in the case of the Elevator Speech, so I put together a method for developing a wardrobe of Elevator Speeches along with a variety of ways to use them in support of career success.

I have a fairly process-oriented mind and see most things as a series of integrated steps. I use the dictionary often as a place to start: grounding myself in exactly "what" is being talking about. When the term "Elevator Speech" starting making its way into my lexicon, I discovered how very little was actually defined; nothing described what an Elevator Speech included or how one is structured.

I took a personal interest in tackling this topic, and I'm glad I did.

In a way, I dedicate this small book to those people out there who wonder what an Elevator Speech really is and how to develop a good one (if not several). Consider this your definitive guide to discovering what an Elevator Speech is, how to construct one, how to use it, and all of the ways you can repurpose it.

To a Powerful Career,
Dorothy

THE INTROVERT WHISPERER™

ELEVATOR SPEECHES that get results

Create a 30-second introduction for greater success

DOROTHY TANNAHILL-MORAN

Introduction to the Elevator Speech

I'M FOCUSING ON the Elevator Speech specifically because it is a tool for representing yourself in a self-introduction. It is also talked about but rarely in terms of how to construct a good elevator speech or pitch. I've created entire workshops around the creation of a good Elevator Speech because it is a vitally important element to the management of your Personal Brand. What I am about to disclose includes everything you need to know about the Elevator Speech.

I will further define what and how to use an Elevator Speech. Contrary to popular belief, an Elevator speech isn't just for job seekers! Everyone in a career of any type needs a good one. This is part of your Personal Brand. This is how you speak about YOU. Therefore, it's good for you to know what it is, how to create a good one, and when to you use it.

So, let's get started.

What is an Elevator Speech?

- The concept of an "elevator speech" is based on a measurement of time. You should be able to articulate your point in the amount of time it takes you to go between floors in an elevator. In other words, about 30 seconds.
- It is a form of self-introduction.

Think of the initial conversation you have with people at a cocktail party, business meeting, or networking event. Usually, the first question you are asked is, "What do you do?"

If done right, an elevator speech can answer the question, "What do you do?" in a more meaningful and lasting way.

The elevator speech answers the "so what" about you and what you do.

IF DONE RIGHT, AN ELEVATOR SPEECH CAN ANSWER THE QUESTION, "WHAT DO YOU DO?" IN A MORE MEANINGFUL AND LASTING WAY.

Too often we simply reply to this question with a job title. Most job titles do nothing to answer the "so what" much less provide anyone with insightful information about the work we do (or our Personal Brand). An Elevator Speech is more than a job title, responsibility, or business. Like your Personal Brand it is also multi-dimensional.

An ES (ES is my shorthand for Elevator Speech) gives the listener a quick understanding of what you bring to the party. It can also help the conversation move more fluidly. Have you ever noticed how right after someone answers the question, "What do you do?" with their title, such as, "I'm an accountant", that the conversation tends to stall out? What can one say after hearing a job title? To make things worse, many job titles are so cryptic that anyone outside of the company where they came from has no clue what the job title means.

DTM (That's me, my initials) thought:

I met a person who introduced himself as "Principal Consultant". Seriously? Do people hear what they say sometimes? While those two words were full of meaning to the man saying them, it said nothing to me or anyone else listening. The dead air space and blank looks told the whole story.

Another way to think about your ES is in terms of using it to serve others. Quickly informing others of what you do in a more meaningful way enables them to more easily tap into your expertise in the future. If you are in job search mode, have a business, or have any career ambitions, you want to present yourself in a professional, credible, and concise manner. What you say needs to be done without boring anyone, without sounding like a sales pitch, and with something memorable or useful.

Keep in mind that you can be clear about your Personal Brand by having a clear ES, giving your network and supporters increased clarity about you. Having a clear ES aids your network in quickly and easily sharing the same juicy nuggets about you with their network. This is primarily how the great opportunity is found. (Here I'm talking about the great job, great new client, great business deal, or great referral.)

Another critical characteristic of your ES is interest. It should be interesting enough to leave the listener begging to know more about you. You can often tell if your ES has impact when someone says, "Really? Tell me more." As I previously mentioned, when you retort back with your job title, the conversation has no-where to go. It's like falling off a cliff; it's abrupt. A good conversationalist keeps the flow of dialogue going.

YOU CAN OFTEN TELL IF YOUR ELEVATOR SPEECH HAS IMPACT WHEN SOMEONE SAYS, "*REALLY?* TELL ME MORE."

Your ES should be said in one or two sentences. You do not want to recite your resume or bore the listener, but rather capture interest and intrigue. Although I said earlier that the ES isn't just for job seekers, I've noticed that when job seekers go to a networking event they tend to cram too much information into their ES. If this is you—stop it!

DTM thought:

WITH AN ELEVATOR SPEECH, *SHORT* IS BEST.

I once met a woman at a networking event for job seekers who, before she even opened her mouth to say anything, indicated with her body language that she was uncomfortable. When she introduced herself, she recited an ES that went on for sentences, even paragraphs. Her ES lasted an eternity! I cringed. What she said sounded like a job description. Since I was at the event to give a career-oriented talk, I took the liberty of giving her some guidance on how to improve her ES. With an ES, short is best.

YOU DON'T WANT TO BE REMEMBERED AS THE PERSON PEOPLE WANT TO AVOID.

Another DTM thought:

In today's fast-paced world, most people would be unable to remain polite to a person who did something like the woman in the story I just told. This woman lacked personal insight. If you find that people abruptly cut you off or glance around, you would do well to look at shortening your ES and conversation responses. You don't want to be remembered as the person people want to avoid.

Let's summarize what we now know about the Elevator Speech:

- It's a self-introduction.
- It's short—1 or 2 sentences at most.
- It's memorable and gives the listener insight into the contributions one makes in one's work.

Personal Branding Statement = Unique Value Proposition = Elevator Speech

FOR SOME REASON, every time a concept becomes popular, people come out of the woodwork with alternates or disparaging remarks about it. I won't try to analyze why this happens but the same is true with the ES; there will always be people who poo-poo the concept by offering up other terminology.

Here is what I have discovered: **These other terms mean the exact same thing.** What's important to grasp is that you are the first person others will hear when they hear about you. What you say when you meet someone creates the all-important first-impression. We tend to think in polar opposites when it comes to the first impression. People think they either have a good impression or a poor one when in actuality the first-impression isn't good or bad but rather memorable or forgettable. Which would you rather have?

If someone has made a compelling argument for disregarding the ES in lieu of some other term, then replace ES for that other term in this book. To me, it is a meaningless distinction. What is more valid than the word used here is your action and ability to say something meaningful in one or two sentences.

An ES is not the beginning of a sales pitch. It's not a pitch at all. Although, you may hear the term "Elevator Pitch" used often interchangeably with Elevator Speech, for sake of clarity, I'm not talking about how to pitch anything to anyone. I believe it could support a sales pitch but that's not the purpose as I outline it.

I will also warn you that you will find numerous articles on this topic in some fairly high profile publications. Just because someone has published an article on the topic doesn't mean that what is outlined is advice you should follow. Many of the articles suggest some cringe-worthy direction on creating an ES, many of which top my list of suggestions to avoid.

Personal Branding 101 and How an Elevator Speech Fits

BY THIS POINT, you have probably picked up on the fact that there is a relationship of some sort between Personal Branding and the ES. And because I'm not going to give you the full-blown Personal Branding education in this book, I suggest you read my other book, *Personal Branding,* to educate yourself fully on the what, why, and how of Personal Branding. (That wasn't really a gratuitous plug even though it kind of sounded like one.) Rather, I think it's important to understand how the various parts of your Career Management strategy fit together.

The best way to think fully about Personal Branding is to think in terms of a multi-faceted prism. Each facet is important to the overall understanding of Personal

Branding and once you comprehend those facets, it will be easier for you to relate this to yourself.

Facet #1: Your Personal Brand is about how you are viewed by others.

Facet#2: Your Personal Brand is how your audience values you.

Facet #3: Your Personal Brand is your reputation.

Facet #4: Your Personal Brand is what is unique about you.

Facet #5: Your Personal Brand is what people come to expect from you.

Facet #6: You can deliberately craft your unique Personal Brand.

Think of yourself as a business or product of one. Your Personal Brand is what people come to understand about you, what they come to expect from you, along with what stands out about you (uniqueness) and the value you bring to them. Yes, at the end of the day, it's all about what you can do for others. Keep this in mind as you move through the rest of this book because your ES is all about what you can do for others.

And who are "they" or "others"? Here I'm referring to your audience. You may think this only applies to hiring managers, but it applies to everyone you work with - past, present and future. If you are a business owner, it's your customer. If you work for someone, it's your employer, manager or executive. Your audience is everyone you know, including your mom.

Your Personal Brand can hurt you or help you toward your career goals based on how other people experience you. In many ways, people you work with may know you the best because you spend so much time together and you have the commonality of your place of work. This allows your co-workers to become exposed to all facets. Your challenge is figuring out how to get your audience acquainted with the multiple dimensions of you.

You will discover that your "hard" skills become less important to your professional success than your relationships. Those relationships will exist both inside and outside your immediate place of business. You must be strongly branded for your audience to provide you with ongoing growth in your career. Think of this as a highly strategic element to your career plan. How will the audience that can provide you with opportunities know what your value is and what makes you unique? When they "get" that about you, your opportunities will abound.

Personal Brand is about the multi-dimensional YOU and how those around you experience you—starting with how you introduce yourself. You can help your audience understand your value to them in less than a minute. You might think that impossible but if radio

YOU CAN HELP YOUR AUDIENCE UNDERSTAND YOUR VALUE TO THEM IN LESS THAN A MINUTE.

and TV advertisements can communicate value in such a short time, you can too. When you get to the section on how to develop your ES you will learn that you can say so much in such a short amount of time without sounding like an ad!

Elevator Speech Tips

I HAVE FOUND THAT the ability to create an ES is improved if you know some helpful tips prior to learning the process. It helps to know upfront the things you want to keep in mind as you are developing your ES.

Here are my suggested tips:

- **Develop at least 3 elevator speeches.**
  You will want to orient yourself differently with different audiences. Think through the various people or groups you meet and what message you want them to have about you. You wouldn't want to introduce yourself the same way to a person at a friend's party as you would at a company business meeting. Remember, you are multi-faceted and it's okay for you to represent yourself in slightly different ways, depending upon with whom you interact.

Example to illustrate my point: I recently went to a weeklong business conference where the attendees included all sorts of business owners in varying stages of growth. It was also a networking and cooperative setting where people genuinely wanted to help each other with their businesses. I decided that for the first half of the week, I would use one ES for myself, and then switch to another ES for the second half. I did this because there were two aspects of my Personal Brand that I wanted to share and I didn't want to stuff my ES with more than one idea about myself and risk it being too long and confusing.

MY FIRST ES:

I help climbing yet introverted leaders find their voice and courage for becoming what they were born to be.

MY SECOND ES:

I teach a form of Body Language called Micro Expressions, which is new to the US and increases a person's Emotional Intelligence and professional results.

Both ES are true for me but trying to incorporate both would have been too long and confusing. Most people can only absorb one point at a time.

- **Write each speech out completely and practice saying it out loud until you have it totally memorized or at least**

can repeat its basic idea. You don't want to sound like you're reading it from a piece of paper.

I keep my ES written down and stashed in different locations, especially in front of my phone, for easy access. I also keep them on a note card and review them prior to events so they are fresh in my mind.

You don't have to repeat each ES perfectly or word-for-word as long as you convey the key points you want to make.

Once you have your ES flushed out, recite it out loud. You'll be surprised at how different phrases can sound when you hear them versus when you read them on paper. If you find yourself stumbling through your ES when you say it out loud, you'll know it isn't ready for prime time.

Once you think you have a few winning Elevator Speeches, try them out on people you know and ask for feedback.

Not everyone is immediately comfortable using an ES as a form of self-introduction. However, the more you do, the more comfortable you will become using them. Keep in mind that you are introducing YOU. You know YOU best. If you're comfortable with YOU, the other person will also be comfortable YOU.

Until you feel confident using an ES, keep yours

to one sentence. Shorter is better, but shorter also flows more easily when spoken out loud.

- **Once you have prepared your ES, you will want to prepare a follow-up response for interested parties.**

  Keep in mind that a well-constructed and delivered ES will intrigue people and inspire them to know more. You will need to have a concise response to, "Really? Tell me more." Your response should be brief but powerful, and on the topic of your ES.

Neuroscience/Neuromarketing? Because It's Key to a Memorable Elevator Speech

OVER THE PAST DECADE, scientists have unearthed a great deal of information about how our brains work. One of the more valuable insights pertains to how we make decisions. Needless to say, the marketing community picked up on and applied these findings to their promotion and sales activities. I believe the marketing community understood many of these things previously, but science expanded their thinking. I'm going to outline some of the basic concepts in order to apply them to the method of creating an ES. This background will help provide an understanding of the "why" and "how" to create an ES.

While I'm not a neuroscientist, nor do I play one on TV, I have studied neuroscience and neuromarketing (how marketers have synthesized the science to make more powerful marketing campaigns). Here are some of the most basic concepts.

Concept #1: New Brain v/s Old Brain

New Brain – logical, practical, rationalizes

Old Brain – emotional, survival based; the place where all decisions are made

To capture and keep someone's attention, you must appeal to the Old Brain. Have you ever had someone tell you about a decision they made and offer a rationale that made no sense? This is how our brain works. We first make a decision that comes from the old-emotional center. Then, our new brain kicks in to wrap a rationale around it.

Unfortunately, our emotions don't always come from a place of logic. All our brain knows is that it made a decision and now it's time to take action aligned to that decision. It "feels" right. We like to think we have good, clear rational thinking when we make decisions but it turns out we aren't really rational at all. The decision comes from emotions, and we all know how logical those can be!

What does this mean for your Personal Brand and your ES? It means you must appeal to the emotions, not logic, of other people. This is part of the "so-what" I talked about earlier. You can outline all kinds of logic to other people, but if it doesn't appeal to their old-emotional brain, the old brain doesn't attach any meaning to it.

Put another way, they won't identify with you when the time comes if they perceive no emotional response from what you've said.

Concept #2: The Old Brain Has Rules

Rule 1: The old brain is self-centered. It thinks only, "What's in it for me?" Better known as WIIFM. The truth is we come into this world with a selfish mindset, and we keep this selfish mindset. To be socially acceptable, we learn how to respond to the needs of others BUT we only do that because we've identified something in doing so that feeds our selfish nature. It's still all about "self".

Rule 2: The old brain likes simple contrast—black and white or old and new.

Rule 3: The old brain likes simple input—simple words, street language.

Rule 4: The old brain likes the beginning and ending of a story but not the middle.

Rule 5: The old brain is triggered ONLY by emotion.

Rule 6: The old brain goes to sleep with the phrase, "I am". This is because the old brain wants to operate on autopilot and not be alert. This phrase tells the old brain "categorize now: no further work required". Once the old brain categorizes you; the old brain goes to sleep. Essentially, the old brain forgets about you. Ugh! For example:

- When you tell someone, *"I'm a Career Coach,"* they immediately form an opinion, right or wrong, and then shut down for any more information.
- *"I am . . ."* shuts off the brain of your audience to any more information. That's why giving a job title is the ***last thing*** you want to share with someone, unless you want to get rid of the other person.
- We are very self-centered and are constantly asking "What's in it for me?" That's why you don't want to use an ES that's about you. Successful Elevator Speeches are about the listener and what's in it for them (or their referrals.) Granted, your elevator speech is about YOU but you need to translate what you do in terms that the other person can relate to as a benefit for them.

SHORT IS BETTER

DTM interpretation:

Short is better, I don't want to hear about you, I want to hear about what you can do for me. Don't bore me with details or technical terminology. If you can give it to me as "scratch and sniff" I will love it.

Concept #3: Don't let the old brain go to sleep

- Don't label yourself. For example, don't say, "I am a career coach" or "I am a project manager". You'll notice that in the two Elevator Speeches I did at the conference, I didn't use the word "am". I didn't allow myself to be categorized or labeled. Avoiding this temptation worked like a charm in that I often had people ask me other questions about the work I did.

- Use powerful verbs that identify what you do. Use verbs to describe your role, like "I help" or "I teach". For many people this can be tricky to distill. I suggest consulting the internet for a list of powerful verbs. Search for verbs that describe the action you perform. Hint: Google "powerful verbs". You will find loads of articles and even a website or two devoted to powerful verbs. I suggest you copy these for future reference and during the creation of your ES.

- Talk about results. Use numbers to quantify or qualify your value. Numbers and statistics automatically give credibility to what is being said. This won't apply to all situations, but adding at least one number to your elevator speech will boost your personal credibility significantly.

- Tell how your results will save time, save money, produce income, make someone

> powerful or successful, or attract customers or a mate. Getting back to my point about being self-centered, our results should benefit the listener in some way. That benefit will almost always fall into one of these areas. If you can show how what you do will deliver on one of these benefits, the person you are talking to will listen!

Now that you've had a brief education in Neuromarketing, you will want to keep these things in mind as you create your ES. I suggest referring back to this section while you are producing your ES to ensure it is as powerful as can be.

Elevator Speech—Before and After

I'M GOING TO GIVE you several examples of ES makeovers to help you understand the difference between a strong and weak message. You may want to use what is provided in this section as the foundation for creating your own ES, using what works for you and making modifications to fit your situation.

MORTGAGE BROKER:

B:

I'm a mortgage broker.
I help people find their dream home.

Not horrible but it labels the person by using "am" with a job title. The brain will go to sleep before it hears the second sentence, which is really pretty good.

A:

I teach people 4 secrets of wealth and cash flow so they can leverage other people's money and hang on to more of their own.

This works because it uses a powerful verb right up front, "teach". This is also good because it includes a number. And it gets even better because it talks about making and saving money!

INSURANCE:

B:

I offer comprehensive financial planning services, including retirement and estate planning.

Although this example avoids the word "am", it is seriously boring and doesn't give any benefit to the listener. It fails to answer the "so what?" It also isn't unique or memorable because it doesn't help me distinguish this person from the other 3,000 planners in the city.

A:

I discover between $10k and $20k my clients didn't know they had in 60 minutes or less.

This starts out with a powerful verb, "discover". It also uses numbers and conveys the benefits of saving money and time. This example is short, sweet, and memorable.

SALES TRAINER:

B:

I run sales training for retail furniture stores.

This example avoids using "am" but doesn't really describe any benefit to anyone. Where would your audience go with this response in a conversation?

A:

We enable our customers to sell 20% more than last year with 25% less visitors—that's more than $40k in additional revenue per visitor.

I love the word "enable". Granted, it sounds a bit like a sales pitch but if you were in sales, you'd want to know what this person does. If you weren't in sales, you might tweak this ES by leaving out the last comment about $40k of revenue. Either way, it is a good use of numbers.

HEALTH TRAINER:

B:

I help people get fit and healthy.

The word "help" is a good verb but way too vague. I find that people in this industry have a tendency to be too high level and vague about what they can do for me. Keep in mind, I'm lazy, I don't want to have to figure out how this work might benefit me. This ES needs to be specific so your listener knows exactly how this person might relate to them or a potential referral.

A:

I teach people how to achieve the body of their dreams by lowering their body fat as much as 20% and achieving their ideal weight in 5 months or less.

Good verb used right up front and this example appeals to many benefits. Nice use of numbers. Finally! A health and fitness person that isn't talking in platitudes.

WEB PROGRAMMER

B:

I'm a web programmer.

Use of the word "am" is bad. This example also only uses the job title and nothing else, making it too easy to go to sleep. It is missing any real work or potential benefit. Let's face it, this is a very typical introduction and it stinks.

A:

I've developed two programs that increase online cash flow by up to 20% in 90 days.

Excellent verb used right up front. This example also includes numbers and conveys the benefit of saving money. This person sounds like someone we should all hire!

There you go. You have several examples to inspire you to create your own ES. Use any of these to get started and replace the words and terms that apply specifically to you and your work.

Creating Your Elevator Speech

NOW I'M GOING to run you through a couple of questions to help you think about the ideas you will want to convey in your ES. To really make this work, jot down as many answers as you can think of. Don't limit yourself by the space I have made available. The biggest issue I see when people are creating their ES is a lack of ideas about the work they do. They think in terms that are what I describe as too high level or vague.

Examples of Vagueness and How to Improve:

Too high level or vague:

I coach people.

This barely says anything. While it's true, no one can relate to this. It doesn't help you understand anything about what the person does, how he or she does it, or the benefit to the listener.

Better, but still too high level:

I coach people to achieve their goals.

What kind of goals? How can anyone relate to this?

Best:

I coach people who intend to be managers and executives on how to make more money and achieve their career dreams.

Excellent! There is a powerful verb right up front and it appeals to the desire for money and power.

Time to Think.

EXERCISE#1: What the old brain wants is the result you have produced for others or your company. What results have you produced? What are your accomplishments in this area?

1. ______________________________

2. ______________________________

3. ______________________________

4. ______________________________

5. ______________________________

EXERCISE #2: How do you differentiate yourself? What's unique about you? What do you do differently than others? Look at your stories, the way you perform your job, your results. Don't think in terms of just the type of job or work you do. There are probably 1000's of people who do the same work but only you have your unique combination of skills, education, and capabilities. List those things that make you stand out.

1. ______________________________

2. ______________________________

3. ______________________________

4. ______________________________

5. ______________________________

EXERCISE #3: Elevator Speech – Based on the previous 2 exercises, write down an ES using some of this content. Remember to use powerful verbs and use some of the examples provided in this book as a guide for creating your own.

The format I've laid out below is essential in creating a powerful ES. Until you have produced and used various Elevator Speeches, stick with this format. When you're ready for the Masters in Elevator Speeches, you can switch the order of this format, but you will always want to use the three elements I have laid out here.

To help you with the creation of your ES, I'm going to take a couple of the examples and break them in to these three components. This way you can more specifically relate to the format to create your own.

> **Example:** *I teach people how to achieve the body of their dreams by lowering their body fat as much as 20% and achieving their ideal weight in 6 months or less.*

Part 1: "I do what" = I teach

Part 2: "To whom?" = people*

Part 3: "And get what kind of results?" = how to achieve the body of their dreams by lowering their body fat by up to 20%, and achieve their ideal weight in six months or less.

* With some Elevator Speeches you may need to be more specific about with whom you are achieving results. With this example, using the term "fat people" might be too rude. I hope you get the idea. Being specific is good but being rude isn't.

> **Example:** *I discover between $10k and $20k my clients didn't know they had in 60 minutes or less.*

Part 1: "I do what" = I discover

Part 2: "To whom?" = my clients

Part 3: "And get what kind of results?" = between $10k and $20k my clients didn't know they had in 60 minutes or less.

Note: This ES contains all three parts but not in the order I have it outlined below. This is what I was referring to earlier about keeping all three elements but using them in different order.

Use this format to help you with the construction:

_____________ / _____________ / ____________________

I DO WHAT? TO WHOM? FOR WHAT KIND OF RESULTS?

1. ____

2. ____

3. ____

4. ____

5. ____

Practice. There is a difference between what we write and how we speak. To finalize your speeches, practice first by reading them out loud. If you need to refine or edit, do so. The next step is to read two to three Elevator Speeches to another person and ask for feedback. Again, take the feedback and edit if you think the suggestion will help make a more impactful speech.

Mix and Match. In creating several Elevator Speeches, it can be handy to develop several versions with each of the three elements, and mix and match them in different combinations. This can create what I call a "wardrobe" of Elevator Speeches.

Define your audience: As I mentioned earlier, you will want to develop several Elevator Speeches based on the audience you will most likely encounter. Now that you have several that sound good, identify with which audience each ES will be best to use. Are there any groups you might be missing an ES for? If so, think through what benefit would be the most

YOU CAN DEVELOP YOUR ELEVATOR SPEECH ANY TIME THE NEED ARISES.

beneficial for that group to hear and develop one or two to use when meeting with those people. Keep in mind that you can develop your Elevator Speech any time the need arises or even on the fly once you get adept at creating them. You want to also keep in mind that your ES should align with the rest of your Personal Brand as you have defined it.

Record and memorize. Lastly, you will want to identify the 3 speeches you feel best about saying and that have the most impact. Write these on note cards and memorize them. Bring your note cards with you to events as a helpful reminder, or tape them near your phone to prompt you when needed.

You did it! You've just created Elevator Speeches to use for reinforcing your Personal Brand and for making a powerful and lasting impression.

Get Free Instant Access to Video series,

**"The 5 Most Common Ways
Introverts Commit Career Self-Sabotage
and How to Avoid Them"**

These videos are designed to accelerate your results
with **ELEVATOR SPEECHES THAT GET RESULTS,**
and are my way of saying "thank you" for purchasing this book.

Brought to you by Dorothy Tannahill-Moran, *The Introvert Whisperer,*
dedicated to unleashing your career potential.

www.introvertwhisperer.com/careergoals

Problem Spots

FOR MANY PEOPLE, creating an Elevator Speech can be a real challenge. That's because many people aren't used to thinking about themselves in this way. Many might think they are tall, quiet, detail-oriented, or a hundred different other things, but rarely do people think in terms of what they do for others, the benefit others can derive, and the value placed on those benefits.

If that is the situation you find yourself in, I understand. I had the same challenge when I started out as a Career Coach, as did most of my clients, including clients who had a heavy-duty marketing background. You'd think marketing experts, who work on branding their clients all day long, would think creating an ES was a snap. But, it's easier to be objective about others than ourselves. Thankfully, creating an ES is a learned skill, which means you're in luck.

Let me encourage you in a couple of ways.

Creating an Elevator Speech is about marketing you. As long as you earn an income from clients or employers, you are marketing yourself. I know for some, the idea of self-marketing is distasteful. It's critical to move past that attitude because it doesn't matter what your professional situation is; marketing yourself is exactly what you're doing. You are marketing yourself if you are looking for a job. You are marketing yourself if you need another customer. You are marketing yourself if you want a promotion. This is a good perspective to have from this point forward.

Also, I would hope this makes you more aware of marketing going forward and how various marketing concepts can apply to your career management.

Practice helps in more than one way. I have suggested several times to practice in order to get comfortable with giving your ES. You will also discover that the more you answer the questions previously outlined and create more speeches, using them will also become easier. You will evolve in this process and naturally become better.

Other Uses for Your Elevator Speech

INCREASINGLY MORE business owners, professionals, and job seekers are catching on to the idea and necessity of having a well-created and impactful Elevator Speech. And after all the time and energy spent in creating and practicing them, many people want to get more use out of them than simply waiting to meet someone new. Repurposing your ES as a vehicle for extending your Personal Brand is a great idea.

Here are some additional uses for your Elevator Speech:

> **Email signature.** Most email services provide users the ability to automatically "stamp" the end of any email with what is called a signature. I have seen an array of signatures, from one that has a simple closing statement and person's name, all the way to multiple links and graphics. Take

advantage of your signature capabilities and include your name, phone number, and ES. If you are concerned that your ES will get old and shop-worn, then simply rotate your ES on some type of schedule, like every 8 weeks. Everyone should have more than one ES and rotating them on your email signature is an easy task.

Business Card. Our business cards have much more real estate available than we use. I'm referring specifically to the back of your card. If your business card is already full of contact information, you should consider having your cards printed up with your primary ES on the back. If there is still room on the front, without looking unprofessional or cluttered, you could put your ES under your name or across the top of the card. Many people make personal notes on business cards to remember things about that new contact. What better way to help everyone who has your business card remember you than by including your ES? If you don't have business cards, you need to get some. Even people who are retired have business cards. It's an easy way to exchange contact information and help people remember you later.

Resume. Your resume is yours to develop as you like; what you put on it is your decision. We know that there are optional elements to your resume, such as a professional summary or objective (usually placed somewhere close to the top under your contact information). You can add your ES either to your professional summary or as the first sentence in your summary. By putting your ES in your resume, you set the tone for how the reader will view your qualifications. You can also use several of them in the professional summary. If you have a resume, you are selling yourself to the resume recipient. They need to know as much about you as possible, especially what you can do for them. This is a place you can use multiple Elevator Speeches very effectively. Of course, you'll want to use a collection of diverse speeches on your resume.

Linked In Profile. I'm listing Linked In specifically because it is the one social media directly oriented to business. Similar to your resume, your Linked In profile reflects your Personal Brand. Take advantage of the exposure and put your ES in your profile. The best place for this is the first comment in the summary section. Placing it here is similar in nature to placing it on your resume in the professional summary. People viewing your profile will read this first, which will set the tone for who you are and what you bring to the party. This will give you more coverage than your experience alone would provide. Also similar to your resume, you can use several Elevator Speeches in your Linked In profile summary.

Social Media. Other than Linked In, your first activity with every other social media platform is to set up your account and create a profile. The amount of profile information available varies from one social media to the next, however each account should contain your ES in your effort to introduce yourself to the people seeing your profile.

Don't be limited to just this list of ES uses. You might have other ideas about where you can use your ES, such as placing it on a website if you have one. Remember, an ES is a form of self-introduction. You don't have to limit its use to saying it out loud anytime you meet someone new in person. And an ES is far more versatile than you might think. Use your ES anywhere you have a profile that introduces you to new people.

More Elevator Speech Tips

BECAUSE I BELIEVE so firmly in the value Elevator Speeches add to our personal and business success, I want to share with you a few more tips. Keep what you like and leave the rest.

Believe it. If you develop an ES that embarrasses you or causes you to cringe, you either need to beef up your confidence or change what you're saying about yourself. Keep in mind that if you don't believe what you are saying, no one else will believe it either.

KEEP IN MIND THAT IF YOU DON'T BELIEVE WHAT YOU ARE SAYING, NO ONE ELSE WILL BELIEVE IT EITHER.

Give it attitude. If your ES lacks energy or enthusiasm, people's response to it will also lack energy or enthusiasm. We like people who have confidence and a bit of attitude toward their abilities. You don't have to brag, but be proud about what you bring to the party. Also, if you find that you are talking yourself out of creating and using an ES *for any reason*, you need a change of attitude. You may feel uncomfortable using your ES until you've practiced enough to get past that feeling. That feeling is NOT necessarily a signal that your ES is wrong for you or your profession. That feeling is simply the result of learning something new. The uncomfortable feeling will pass but only if you practice delivering your ES long enough for it to.

Smile. It's hard not to love people who smile. A smile communicates warmth and confidence. A smile helps you come across as engaging and inviting. People want to know more about people who smile.

Shut up. Once you've delivered your ES, stop yourself from saying anything else. I know this is a tough one, but people often deflate the impact of their ES by blathering on afterward. When you stop talking, it will also prompt your listeners to ask about you or introduce themselves. Both results are great.

Leave them wanting more. One way to test the power of an ES is to see if the listeners ask you more about what you've just said. Have fun with this. The next time you attend a professional meeting, articulate your ES and then just be quiet and see what happens next.

Use it all the time. Use your ES every time you introduce yourself. Use it during 1:1 introductions or in group settings. Use it in professional settings or personal settings. Use your ES everywhere people don't already know you.

Understand and articulate what is unique about you. If you do nothing else, spend time truly understanding what differentiates you; what causes you to stand out. This is what you want in your ES, so make sure you articulate it clearly.

Practice until it rolls off your tongue. Write down your ES and practice it until it becomes second nature to you. This will result in a confident appearance when you say it.

Think short and sweet. One sentence is usually enough. Powerful is not lengthy or wordy. Forcing your ES into one single sentence causes you to think about each word more carefully and choose those that convey the most about you.

Use a verb as your second word. What do you do? What do you do for others? Using a verb as your second word helps you think about your results and accomplishments in concrete terms. Get a list of powerful verbs. Look them up. Use them.

7 Issues to Avoid with Your Elevator Speech

WE ALL KNOW WE need an ES, especially if we're a job seeker or a business owner. An ES can be a great and memorable way to introduce ourselves, if done right. When elevator speeches go wrong, they are memorable for the wrong reasons – mostly they're boring or cringe-worthy.Don't let that be you.

> **WHEN ELEVATOR SPEECHES GO WRONG, THEY ARE MEMORABLE FOR THE WRONG REASONS— MOSTLY THEY'RE BORING OR CRINGE-WORTHY.**

Here are 6 of the more common issues you want to avoid in creating your ES.

1. **Waaaay too long.** I have heard Elevator Speeches that were longer than commercials. While it may be tempting to put a full-length resume into an ES for a quick oral review, don't do it. Make your ES a maximum of 1 or 2 sentences in length. In the case of Elevator Speeches—less is more.
2. **Overly-used terms.** Just as you need to avoid certain overly-used and trite terms in your resume or social media, you'll want to avoid those same terms in your ES. Terms like "customer service oriented", "people person", and "results oriented" need to be kept out of the ES. Use a more powerful and specific vocabulary.
3. **Wimpy words.** Instead, use powerful verbs. Think about your results, and if you can toss in numbers or comparisons you've hit gold. They all add to increased credibility.
4. **Starting with "I am".** Starting an ES with "I am" is like hitting the snooze button on your alarm clock. The primitive brain of your listener will go into autopilot. "I am" allows the brain to instantly categorize you and go to sleep. Your ES should be interesting and compelling enough to make the listener want to ask more about you because they can't engage with you after they've checked out.

   You may want to gravitate back to using "I am" because it's easy and comfortable. However, you will become equally comfortable not using "I am" after enough practice. The latter will eventually become second nature. Also, keep in mind that you are doing yourself and everyone you know a disservice by not helping them understand clearly how you can serve them.

5. **The cringe-factor.** I've heard some Elevator Speeches that made me cringe with embarrassment. The person saying it made up something, but I could tell it wasn't something they were comfortable with. You do have to practice your ES until you become comfortable with it. If you still feel like you have fleas in your shorts after you've memorized it, then you may need to toss it out and start over again. Your ES needs to be worded in a way that you feel comfortable and even proud to say. It should reflect your authentic self.

6. **Not compelling.** It is kind of tough to think about ourselves in glowing, interesting terms. But you only have one opportunity to make a first impression on someone and hold their attention. I have yet to meet someone who didn't have at least one seriously interesting thing to say about him or his business. Focus on that one seriously interesting thing about yourself in your ES. If you can't think of anything, you haven't thought hard enough. If you still can't think of anything, ask people you know to tell you what sorts of things they tell

> **YOU ONLY HAVE ONE OPPORTUNITY TO MAKE A FIRST IMPRESSION ON SOMEONE AND HOLD THEIR ATTENTION.**

people about you. Their responses may be memorable and compelling.

7. **Starts with an agenda.** This issue could warrant its own chapter. Keep in mind that you are introducing yourself as the first step in building a relationship with someone. Anytime you start making demands of a relationship before investing the time needed to develop that relationship, you set yourself up for failure. Starting with an agenda is a signal to your listener that you are focusing on your own goals. This could result in the listener feeling like they are being used. There is an "emotional bank account" we all must place deposits in first, (friendship, support, goodwill) before we can take withdrawals (favors, requests, asks). It's called reciprocity. Do not attempt to set up your ES as a sales pitch unless the agenda is established expressly as such.

You don't want to be on the receiving end of an ES that you want to run away from. More importantly you don't want that emperor of the ES coming out of you. Keep these tips in mind; and you will have an ES that makes a lasting impression.

Conclusion

THAT'S IT! You now know all there is to know about this subject and are fully equipped to make as many Elevator Speeches as you will ever need.

Your ES is one of the tools you need to have in your Career Management toolkit. As with any tool, you need to put it to use, which is the only way it will serve you.

You may discover while going through this book that you can apply what you've learned to other aspects in your Career. It's no coincidence. I have found that many elements in both marketing and sales can apply to what we need to do to be successful in our chosen field of work. Certainly, this applies to those who own their own business but it also applies to everyone who works for someone else. We went to school to learn specific skills and it is only through our own personal marketing of those skills we are able to have them gainfully deployed.

All the best,
Dorothy

A PERSONAL NOTE

My mission is to help as many people as I can love the work they do and successfully do it. How can I help you be more successful? I'd love to hear from you. If you'd like to share your ES with me for my feedback, or have a troublesome work issue I can help with, please email me at:

Dorothy@introvertwhisperer.com

PS: Please post an honest review of this book.

VIDEO SERIES

Get Free Instant Access to Video series,

"The 5 Most Common Ways Introverts Commit Career Self-Sabotage and How to Avoid Them"

These videos are designed to accelerate your results with **ELEVATOR SPEECHES THAT GET RESULTS,** and are my way of saying "thank you" for purchasing this book.

www.introvertwhisperer.com/careergoals

WOULD YOU PLEASE REVIEW?

WOULD YOU BE so kind as to leave a book review? Authors' books have a much better chance at being successful when our readers share that they enjoyed reading the book and/or found it helpful . . . which I hope you did. If you could take a few minutes to leave a review, I'd appreciate it ever so much.

RESOURCES

BOOKS

The following books provide great insight into how our brain works when making decisions or Neuroscience:

Sway: the Irresistible Pull of Irrational Behavior
by Ori Brafman and Rom Brafman

Neuromarketing: Understanding the "Buy Buttons" in Your Customers Brain
by Patrick Renvoisse and Christophe Morin

The Buying Brain: Secrets for Selling to the Subconscious Mind
by Dr. A K Pradeep

How We Decide
by Jonah Lehrer

Made to Stick: Why Some Ideas Survive and Others Die
by Chip Heath and Dan Heath.

RESOURCES

VERB LISTS

The following are articles you can reference to obtain powerful verbs. As with everything out on the Internet, things come and go. I try to ensure my resources are accurate and relevant, please understand some of these resources may no longer exist by the time you attempt access.

https://www.themuse.com/advice/185-powerful-verbs-that-will-make-your-resume-awesome

http://salt.arizona.edu/sites/salt.arizona.edu/files/tutoringfiles/handouts/Powerful%20Verbs%20for%20Essays.pdf

http://vspa.berkeley.edu/sites/vspa_space/files/shared/doc/LIST-OF-STRONG-VERBS.doc

OTHER BOOKS FROM DOROTHY TANNAHILL-MORAN

Career Mapping:
Planning Your Career on Purpose

Easier Networking
for Introverts and the Socially Reluctant:
A 4-Step Guide That's Natural, Stress-Free and Gets Results

Personal Branding:
A Simple Guide to Reinvent & Manage Your Brand
for Career Success

Accelerate your Career
(Even with a Bad Boss):
A New Approach to Managing Up

ABOUT THE AUTHOR

Dorothy Tannahill-Moran is *The Introvert Whisperer,* a leadership and career coach, author and speaker. Born an introvert, then shaped into a leader, she is a delightful fusion of unique, useful insight and rock-solid management expertise. As a Career Coach, she guides the reluctant toward better relationships with their boss and management, teaching introverts how to effectively collaborate with difficult people, navigate workplace culture and internal politics, and successfully network in a room filled with strangers. This is why Dorothy Tannhill-Moran is a sought-out and trusted advisor to corporate professionals and executives worldwide.

A graduate of Emporia State University with a Bachelor of Science in Education, Dorothy was recruited by the Kansas City School District to coordinate their Distributive Education program. Four years later, she was hired by Intel where she quickly rose through their ranks to senior-level management. With over twenty-one years supervising Intel's diverse staff mix, she coached, guided and trained others at all levels to achieve impressive careers, executive status, higher salaries, while gaining broad professional recognition. Twice, Intel bestowed upon her their highest achievement award, spotlighting her outstanding accomplishments and the positive, long-lasting impact she made on their culture.

For more powerful career strategies, go to:
www.introvertwhisperer.com

Made in the USA
Las Vegas, NV
19 December 2021